Wall of Fire and Glory

The Divine Refiner's Instrument

Wall of Fire and Glory

The Divine Refiner's Instrument

Fidel Ugbo

&

Ben Bethel

EXCELLER BOOKS™
A GLOBAL PRESS

Wall of Fire and Glory

The Divine Refiner's Instrument

Cover design by Exceller Books using resources from Pixabay.com

ISBN: 978-81-19524-79-2

First published in India in 2024 by Exceller Books,
An Imprint of GE Group

Address: G1, Dream Apartment, Degree College Road, Belgharia,
Kolkata, 700056, India

EXCELLER BOOKS™
A GLOBAL PRESS

www.excellerbooks.com

Dedication

We dedicate this book to God, the Father, for His compassionate heart in sending His only begotten Son, Jesus, to come and die on account of our sins. We also dedicate it to our Lord and Savior, Jesus Christ, for accepting to die for our sins and who, by His Spirit, had convicted us to be transformed.

And to the Holy Spirit, who has been with us since Jesus brought us to the Father, giving us more reasons for living and carrying out the work of our Father. This revelation from His word was only possible with the leading of the Holy Spirit.

We also dedicate the work to our precious wives and children for their Love, forbearance and encouragement that have contributed to the penning down of this material.

Acknowledgement

First and foremost, we express our deep gratitude to our LORD and Savior, Jesus Christ, for his wonderful works of salvation for humanity. We also bless the name of the Lord for the support from both our families, who have been pillars behind all our success and that of the Ministry. Our special thanks and appreciation also goes to all servants of God who contributed in one way or the other toward the compiling of this treasurable material.

We must remember Apostle B.E. Okenwa of Jesus Reigns Ministry, Lusiana, USA, for releasing a prophetic word about the writing of this material. We also remember God's General David MWAKPA of Assemblies of God ECKARATH DUSSEDORF Germany for preparing a platform and giving Apostle Bethel the opportunity to minister on this subject in Germany. We love you all.

We also acknowledge Rev. Dr Apostle TAMBE of the Apostolic Mission, Cameroon, Rev. Paul Tom KAMGHA of the Apostolic Mission, Paknor of the Full Gospel Mission Cameroon and my beloved younger brother Innocent AJANAKEM. Barrister MIKE and Justice Verrangasa of Faith Bible Church Kumba. Also worthy of mention are Rev. and Mrs AYuk Rapheal and the members of the Haggai Alumni of Cameroon. God bless you all.

Table of Contents

Introduction

The Bible explains to us that the reason God's own children (Christians) are perishing is because of a lack of knowledge (divine revelation on the subject of Christianity). Not only that, the scripture continues by saying it is not only because they lack knowledge but because of their vehement, deliberate inability, through laziness and carelessness, to study and have a deeper understanding of what God is saying concerning the Cross and the Throne.

"My people are destroyed for lack of knowledge: because thou hast rejected knowledge, I will also reject thee, that thou shalt be no priest to me: seeing thou hast forgotten the law of thy God, I will also forget thy children."

Hosea 4:6

So, the masterpiece you have in your hands, **'WALLS OF FIRE AND GLORY'** comes in to guide our understanding of how God uses fire as a tool to prune the lives of those who are separated unto him through salvation in Christ Jesus. And, also to know how to present ourselves to God for divine transformation through his Word which has the ability to build us up and give us an inheritance amongst them that are sanctified by faith.

Acts 20:32

It is worth noting that this book is not just an ordinary circular novel but a message inspired from above to change our lives so that we can change our generation. Halleluiah, praise the Lord!

Chapter| 1
Roundabout Protection

He wants to show His mercy to His people. When we are born again, supernatural changes take place in our lives as Christians. We receive divine protection from our Almighty Father. In the book of Zechariah, the word of God tells us that the Lord will be unto the church a wall of fire and glory, which means, therefore, that our precious heavenly father is mindful of our security.

"For I", saith the Lord, "will be unto her a wall of fire round about and will be the glory in the midst of her."

"Ho, ho come forth and flee from the land of the North, Saith the Lord, for I have spread you abroad as the four winds of the heavens saith the LORD."

Zechariah 2:5-6

"So, brethren, if you have been pursued by demons all through your life, we advise that you get up today and enjoy the protection that God has given you by taking advantage of His awesome presence in your life. God told Abraham, your friends shall be my friends, and your enemies shall be my enemies. He who blesses you shall be blessed, and he who curses you shall be cursed" (Genesis 12:3). That is the reason we have been seriously affirming to Christians that they are not living their lives at the mercy of the devil. This is because a lot of Christians in the New Testament still believe that the devil is ruling over their lives.

Wrong doctrinal teachings have kept people that God has liberated by the death of His son, Jesus Christ, to remain in bondage. Some people believe that the ruler-ship of the devil over the world is so invincible, but we want to discredit it here because it is a fallacy. The devil's rulership, even in the Old Testament, ended up at the level of the prince. The devil has never been the king of the world. The Bible addresses him as the prince of this world. Even Jesus Christ said,

"The prince of this world cometh but have nothing in me"

John14:30

"And, the word of God explains to us that God has by the death of Jesus on the cross of Calvary made us kings and priests to reign on earth."

Revelation 5:10

"He that dwelled in the secret place of the Most High shall abide under the shadow of the Almighty. I will say of the Lord; he is my refuge and my fortress: my God in Him will I trust. Surely He shall deliver thee from the snares of the fowler and from the noisome pestilence.

He shall cover thee with His feather, and under to his wings shall thou trust His truth, which shall be thy shield and buckler.

Thou shall not be afraid the terror by night nor for the arrows that flight by day:

Nor for the pestilence that walketh in darkness or for the destruction that wasted at noonday.

A thousand shall fall at thy side and ten thousand at thy right hand, but it shall not come nigh thee.

Only with thine eyes shalt thou behold and see the reward of the wicked.

Because thou hast made the Lord which is my refuge even the most high thy habitation.

There shalt no evil befall thee, neither shall any plague come nigh thy dwelling."

Psalm 91: 1-10

The Psalmist explains to us God's protection in the lives of those who dwell in His secret place, which is His awesome presence. When you find your habitation within the walls of fire, his ever-abiding glory shall envelop you and ensure your security.

In the book of Chronicles, the Bible says that glory and honour are in his presence. This explains to us that when we make up our minds to dwell in God's presence every day of our lives, we shall walk in glory and honour.

Glory and honour are in His presence; strength and gladness are in his place.

I Chronicles 16:27

When we consistently dwell in God's presence not only shall we inherit glory and honor but strength and gladness shall be our inheritance. When we get His strength we shall be full of power to do exploits.

In Deuteronomy 5:24, the Bible says, "And ye said behold the LORD our God hath shown us His glory and His greatness. And we have heard His voice out of the midst of fire. We have seen this day that God doth talk with man and he liveth".

There are certain things that we become beneficiaries of when we are encamped around the wall of fire or when we are in God's presence. He will show us His glory and greatness. We will also have access to His voice, which will enable us to walk in His will for us.

The Lord said to Isaiah, "For thus has the Lord spoken unto me, like as the lion and the young lion roar on his prey. When a multitude of shepherds is called forth against him, he will not be afraid of their voices nor abase himself for their noise: so shalt the Lord of hosts come down to fight for Mount Zion and for the hills thereof.
As birds fly, so will the Lord of Host defend Jerusalem. He will also deliver it and pass it over; he will preserve it."

Isaiah 31: 4-5

The Lord is still here assuring his children of His protection when they keep acknowledging his supremacy over their affairs of life. As a Christian, the wall of fire is giving you roundabout protection, but you must separate yourself from the land of the North (known as the Land of sin) and totally concentrate yourself on divine services. Your total concentration has to be on God and on Him alone.

"I will lift up mine eyes unto the hills from whence cometh my help; my help cometh from the Lord which made heaven and earth.
He will not suffer thy feet to be moved: he that keepeth thee will not slumber.
Behold he that keepeth Israel shalt neither slumber nor sleep.
The Lord is thy keeper, and the Lord is thy shed upon the right land.
The sun shall not smite thee by day or the moon by night.
The Lord shall preserve thee from all evil: he shall preserve thy Soul.
The sun shall not smite thee by day nor the moon by night.
The Lord shall preserve thee from all evil; he shall preserve thy soul; the Lord shall preserve thy going out and thy coming in from this time forth and even forever more."

Psalms121:1-8

The Bible tells us that the Lord surrounds His people in the same way that Jerusalem is surrounded by mountains, which means He is mindful of protecting us and giving us a peaceful living here on earth. If you have been living in fear, we want to announce to you that the protection of God is over you and your entire household.

His Word as Fire into Your Unique Purpose

"'Is not my word like fire?' Saith the Lord and like a hammer that breaketh the rock in pieces?"

Jeremiah 23:29

God's word like fire can illuminate your life and destiny and can also break every Iron Gate that has been standing on your way to hinder your purpose, if only you discover the reality of its infallibility and key into it prophetically. The word of God can light your path and lead your way only when you understand it and walk according to its principles.

No wonder the Psalmist says, "Thy word is a lamp unto my feet and a light unto my path" Psalm I19:I05

Then the word of the Lord came unto me saying, "Before I formed thee in the belly, I knew thee, and before thou camest out of the womb, I sanctified thee and ordained thee a prophet unto the nations."

Jeremiah I:4-5

God did not photocopy you out of your parents, but it was His original designation for you to come to this world through them as human channels. That is why you discover that a rich young man testifies that he was brought to this world through a very wretched couple, but destiny has got him wealthy. The simple reason is that his destiny was not founded in the womb. The womb here was just a resting place in his journey of life. Brother, you did not actually come from the womb as you may think. Your destiny, life and purpose existed before the womb. God had already destined you for a specific assignment to be fulfilled on planet Earth before you came here.

That is to say, you are not merely a product of your father's sperm box and your mummy's womb like any other animal could be. Rather, you are God's workmanship created in Christ Jesus unto good works, which God has before ordained, and we should walk in them. (Ephesians'2:9-10)

God told Jeremiah "Before I formed you in the belly" which means, you were actually formed in your mother's womb by God and not by your father's sperms and He already had something good in His mind towards you before he brought you forth to this word. All you need to do is to listen to Him as Jeremiah did and build more confidence in Him who is able to bring you into the fullness of your earthly assignment and purpose.

One serious problem that over 70% of the world's population is yet to arrive at its solution is the answer to this question: "What in this frustrating world am I here for?" However, the answer to this question, having been a hidden treasure to the understanding of many, has made a lot of people live with the delusion and negative impression that they were just a product of a biological accident and that they are just here to see off others. Be assured that this is not true about your life because you are a divine assignment going somewhere to be fulfilled or a miracle going somewhere to happen. However, you must search out the purpose of your existence, or you will never live a glorious life here on earth, and life is going to deprive you of many opportunities, advantages and enjoyment. The Bible says:

"It is the glory of God to conceal a thing, but the honour of kings is to search out the matter."

Proverb 25:2

The real things of your destiny may be hidden from your understanding but today we want to let you know that it your personal responsibility to search them out. When you succeed to understand them, take hold of them and do not let them go.

Some people will be anxious to ask how these things can be or how they can discover what they were sent to this world to do. We hereby offer you the answer to that: You need to be transformed by the spirit of God, or you need to be born again. And when you become a Christian, you don't just take it easy business with God, but you continue to seek Him until your path is made clear and brighter by Him for you to walk in it. Get by the Holy Spirit to a realm where you can understand and approve things that God destroys for your life and purpose.

Paul, the apostle in the book of Acts 26:18-26 was able to analyze with real-life facts what God's purpose for him was because he lived an effective Spiritual life. So he could dictate from the realm of the spirit where he came from what package God had for him there and towards the earth. So, this matter concludes that your life originated from the realm of the spirit, and you have to be very spiritual in order to know what you are here for. Because if you do not know why you are here, you will not know where you are coming from and eventually will lack the knowledge of where you are going, and this will render you purposeless.

The only thing that can give you the knowledge of why you are here is when you appropriately understand where you are coming from and where you are going. Praise the Lord, Brethren! Don't accept to live purposelessly.

Chapter| 2

Purifying to Perfection
(The Cleansing power of God's Word)

"But who may abide on the day of his coming? And who shall stand when he appears? For he is like a refiner's fire and like fuller soap. And he shall sit as a refiner and PURIFIER of silver, and he shall purify the Sons of Levi and purge them as gold and silver so that they may offer unto the Lord an offering in RIGHTEOUSNESS."

Malachi 3: 2-3

The word of God lets us know that we are a special group of super humans created and called by God for a unique purpose.

But ye are a chosen generation, a royal priesthood, a holy nation, a peculiar people, that ye should show forth the praises of him who hath called you out of darkness into his marvellous light.

I Peter 2:9

From the above passages, we are made to fully understand that we are God's project on earth. The reason He gave His first begotten son to come and die the death of a sinner was that He may by the cross give His life in exchange for ours so that He could present to His Father, a sin-free people with a purposeful living. He did not just die because He wanted you to become a religious church-goer. It was to make your person full of glory and excellent living.

But in order for you to attain this level of greatness, you must be willing to pass through the refiner's workshop so that any useless particle can be eliminated from you and you may become useable of the Lord. From our opening scripture, the word of God tells us that God is a refiner and that He is set to purify all the sons of Levi as silver and gold so that they can offer acceptable and righteous sacrifices unto Him, which means we are not supposed to be in a hurry for God to use us. We are supposed to wait until He confirms to us that his refining, purifying and transforming plan for our lives is complete.

The fact that you are born again does not mean that because you are already acceptable as beloved, you have immediate access to the kingdom's physical property. Yes, God has blessed us with all spiritual blessings in heavenly places in Christ, but it takes a spiritual man for all these blessings to manifest in the physical world. God cannot open doors of physical, financial and material blessings to crude and unrefined, unpunctual or natural man because this kind of untransformed person will use God's blessings to fulfil his carnal desires. For example, just think of what is going to happen to a Christian who is still attending nightclubs. If he happens to have ten million francs or dollars in his account, he will make sure that he drinks out himself with all the money, but a transformed, refined and a kingdom conscious Christian will use such money for the glory of the Lord, which means until God finishes His cleansing, refining and transforming project in your life, you are bound to remain a financial liability. He is a vigilant and calculative investor who will never invest in unbroken, uncultured and untransformed vessels.

God will always invest in people who will use the blessing to offer righteous sacrifices to Him and not blemish ones, and for any Christian to be able to offer unbendable sacrifices unto the Lord, he/she must pass through the spiritual refinery.
No wonder the Bible says,

"When the Lord shall build up Zion, He shall appear in His Glory. He shall answer the prayers of the destitute and not despise their prayers."

Psalms 102: 16-17

This means God is not only interested in answering any kind of prayer. You may pray from now till eternity without receiving any answer to your prayer, not because He is wicked to you but because He wants you to be mature enough to handle what you are praying for. So, what we are implying here is that your prayers are useless until you fully allow God to work in your life and remove all the anti-prosperity issues that are still living in you.

"Is not my word like a fire? Saith the Lord; and like a hammer that breaketh the rock in pieces?"

Jeremiah 23:29

The description given to God's word here as fire suggests that Gods word has the distinctive ability to burn out every filthiness from the sons of Levi (Christians) and as hammer means it has the ability to break every stony heart and bring it to its original place in God's will. From our opening scripture we learn that God Himself will sit down as a refiner and a purifier to carry on the work himself in the lives of the sons of Levi.

We want you to know what Levi theologically represents in the Bible. Levi was the third son of Jacob, and God chose his descendants, formally known as the priests and the Levites. It was only from the family of Levi that God authorized people to offer sacrifices to him, and the Bible says, "Ye are a chosen generation, a royal priesthood", which means Christians are the priests and the Levites of this generation and the Bible says that before the priests and the Levites could offer acceptable and righteous sacrifices to God, He would have to purge them as gold that is nothing without the refinery.

Little wonder the word of God tells us that Nadab and Abihu died because they offered strange fire to the Lord. (Leviticus 10:1) They were trying to offer sacrifice to the Lord by fire, while the fire of the Lord hadn't worked in them enough to qualify them to operate in that office. Take note that these two guys were born sons of Aaron, and right, they were supposed to offer sacrifices because they were from the family of Levi from where God originally ordained priests and Levites to function, but they got it wrong because their lives were still not transformed enough to get them qualified for such duties.

That is the simple reason why Christians have been releasing fire into the Camp of the enemy, and it has been coming back to them. This will continue to happen because they still have some untransformed parts in their lives that the purifying fire of God's word has not finished its duties in them. So, we rather advise Christians to submit to the voice of the Lord through the scripture because that is what will make them emerge winners and conquerors without stress.

For all scripture is given of God, and it is profitable for doctrine to reproof, correct, and instruct in righteousness. That the man of God may be perfect thoroughly furnished unto all good works.

II Timothy 3:16

So when you fully submit to the doctrine, reproof, correction, and instruction that God is giving to you through the scripture, you will be perfectly finished with all good works. This means the word of God, when totally yielded to, will become profitable for you in your spiritual life, physical, material and financial living that almost every Christian is longing after, for the word of God is able to build you up and give you victory amongst the sanctified ones.

This does not at all mean that when you became a newborn baby in Christ, you needed to do something for yourself. All you need to do is to be obedient and active over every word that God speaks to you, either by your pastors or from the scripture, because that is the only way you can become mature enough to claim the promises of God in your life. You must always remember that no matter how intensive your problems and weeping may be, God cannot bypass His principles that govern blessings to give you what you will not be able to control.

The Bible

says that as long as the heir is a child, he is no different from a servant, even though he is Lord of all. He is under tutors and governors until the time appointed by the father.

Galatians 4:1-2

This passage of the Bible tells you that divine heritage can never be handed to spiritual children. So you have to arrive at the time appointed by the Father (time of maturity) before anything can be handed over to your care. After God has purified and refined you, you will have the boldness to stand in His presence when He appears in the congregation of the Saints. You will be like Moses when God appears. He was allowed to loiter to him in His presence, but the children of Israel were terribly afraid of His voice and presence. You will have boldness because your master God has purged you to look like Him.

"Herein is our love perfected, so that we may have confidence in the day of judgment; because as he is, so also are we in this world.
There is no fear in love, but perfect love casteth out fear because fear has torment; he that fear is not made purged in Love."

I John 4:17-18

This portion of the scripture clarifies to us that the people who can stand God's presence are people Who have already finished his refining, purifying, and transformation work in their lives. The reason the opening scripture of this chapter began with a question, "But who may abide the day of his coming? And who shall stand when he appears?" is because all the sons of Levi were filthy and for them to gain boldness to minister in God's presence, He had to purge, cleanse, purify, refine and justify them before they can gain boldness to stand and minister in His presence. This was a picture of our initial state in Christ, but His responsibility was to cleanse and sanctify us by the washing of water by the word of God in His mouth that He may present us to the Father, a glorious people without spots, wrinkles and blemishes.

"The wicked flee when no man pursues them, but the righteous are bold like lions."

Proverbs 28:1

Only the righteous will be bold to stand in the presence of the Lord when He appears, but the wicked will flee away from His presence for fear of figment. So, brothers, make yourselves available for the refining and cleansing power of His word to work in you so that you may have the boldness to approach the throne of grace in prayers, having confidence that He will answer your prayers because they are done in His will: Praise the Lord!

Chapter| 3
The Wilderness Experience

"All the commandments which I command thee this day shall ye do that ye may live and multiply and go and possess the land which the Lord God sware unto your fathers.

And thou shall remember all the ways which the Lord thy God led thee these forty years in the WILDERNESS to HUMBLE thee and to prove thee to know what was in thine heart, whether wither thou wouldest keep his commandments or not.

And he humbled thee with Manna which thou knewest knavest not neither did thy father know that he might make thee know that Man doth not live by bread only but by every word that proceeded out of the mouth of the Lord.

Thy raiment's warred no oid upon thee; neither did thy foot swell these forty years.

Thou shall considerer in theme heart that as a man chastened his Son, so the LORD thy God chastened thee."

Deuteronomy 8:1-5

There is one thing that is inevitable in life. This one thing is the wilderness experience, which constitutes the pruning season in one's Christian life. As a Christian or a child of God who is hanging on to attain perfection, it is required that an accurate understanding of God's word as far as advancing in God's kingdom or progressing in Christian life is concerned should be highly assimilated and understood. It is very obvious that so many Christians, because of a lack of a deeper understanding of God's word, have gone about with erroneous beliefs and allusions. So many Christians believe that when they are faced with a difficult situation, they can force God or rather bribe God to take them out of such situation through fasting and prayers. Some ignorantly attribute any seeming failure of theirs to be an attack from the kingdom of darkness as if God has slept and slumbered as far as protecting them is concerned. Those are carefully believed by a lot of Christians in God's kingdom.

"For I, saith the LORD, will be unto her a wall of fire round about and will be the glory in the midst of her.

Ho, ho, come forth, and flee from the land of the north, saith the Lord, for I have spread you abroad as the four winds of the heavens saith the Lord."

Zechariah 2:5-6

Listen here, oh you, simple and hard to understand what the Lord is saying about you that have escaped the land of the north (Barbaric or sinful land) to righteousness is; **"I will be a wall of fire to you"**, which means His protection is everlasting in your life. So, the belief that the devil always eats when the Lord is not there is falsehood and also that all difficulties that come from the devil are blatant lies from the pit of hell. So, the wilderness experience or pruning season is inescapable, though it is a frowning season in everyone's life who has ever had such an experience.

Our opening scripture in this chapter teaches us that the Israelites' forty years of experience in the wilderness was merely to humble them so that when they eventually receive the promised land, they will treat the inheritance with reference to God, respect and fear of Him that had given them the power to conquer seven dangerous nations in their land of promise (Jericho).

The talks of reaching the whole world with the gospel of Jesus must be done in humility. Every vessel that must work with God in the move must be refined because self or carnality has no part to play in this issue.

"Verily verily, I say unto you, except a corn of wheat fall into the ground and die it abideth alone. But if it dies, it brings forth many fruits."

John 12:24

The importance of the wilderness experience is that it makes one dead to self, and the flesh is programmed to work in accordance with the leadership of the spirit. When God wants to enthrone you, He must prune you and humble you in the wilderness. There is really no elevation without humility, no crown without the cross. So you better go through the cross and inherit the crown because praying against the cross is equally praying against the crown or enthronement.

When we consciously go through the wilderness knowing where we will end up, it enables us to become pliable and useful materials in the hands of the transformer, and when it is complete from the inside, the outside will experience the glory. So don't be in haste to give up. Because your prayer has not been answered, keep on; your desire should not be cut short. When God wants to anoint a man or woman, He makes sure that such a person is broken in the flesh in order to be alive in the spirit, and the flesh can only be broken through the wilderness experience or the pruning season. God cannot deposit His power upon unbroken vessels (those not purified by the Gospel), so the only way up is to humble yourself and go down to the lowest. In the wilderness experience, God shatters your dependence on your own strength and brings you to a place of total dependence on

Him. He also cautions Christians from idolizing their gifts, talents, and abilities.

Looking back to what the book of John 12:24 says, we discover that the wilderness experience will enable a Christian to be dead to self so that God can be totally enthroned in his/her life.

I am crucified with Christ; nevertheless, I live, yet not I, but Christ lives in me, and the life which I now live in the flesh, I live by the faith of the son of God, who loved me and gave himself for me.

Galatians 2:20

The apostle Paul here shows us that for us to be alive in Christ, we must be totally dead to our self-will, anxieties, and fleshly desires. God cannot pour out His blessings upon someone whose flesh has not been slain. Even Jesus Christ, the first begotten of the Father, did not do otherwise. In order for Him to take the place of the Father in the kingdom, He had to be slained.

"And I beheld, and I heard the voice of many angels round about the throne and the beast and the elders, and their numbers were ten thousand times ten thousand and thousands of thousands.

Saying with a loud voice, worthy is the lamb that was slain to receive power, riches, wisdom, strength, honour, glory and blessings."

Revelation 5:11-12

All these gifts that are enumerated above were in the custody of the Father but the son had to be slained to receive them. This means there is much for you in God's store room but He wants you to be slained in the flesh before you can receive them.

Blessed be the God and the Father of our Lord who had blessed us with all spiritual blessings in heavenly places in Christ.

Ephesians I:3

Literally, this scripture says that God has already blessed us. It doesn't say He was going to bless us. This means when you receive Christ into your life, you become a blessed man or woman from that day, but the blessings are spiritual, and God wants to use the wilderness experience to work out your life to a platform where you can be able to have access to the blessing He has given you in the physical world.

"But now, thus says the LORD, that created thee, O Jacob, and he that formed thee, O Israel. Fear not, for I have redeemed thee; I have called thee by thy name; thou art mine.

When thou passest through the waters, I will be with thee, and through the rivers, they shall not overflow thee. When thou walkest through the FIRE, thou shall not be burnt; neither shall the flame kindle against thee."

Isaiah 43:I-2

What a glorious and precious thing to hear the Almighty God addressing His kids with such honour. Halleluiah! Praise the Lord; can you, for a minute, worship the Lord before you continue reading? You just heard God's voice saying when you are passing through the waters He will be there with you. What a glorious testimony to hear that our Almighty father is with us in all our life challenges.

No wonder David could speak with such an enormous boldness. He must have understood this mystery.

Yea, though I walk through the valley of the shadow of the death, I will fear no evil, for thou art with me. Thy rod and thy staff, they comfort me.

Psalms 23: 4

Never think that you were found in a difficult moment because God abandoned you to the devil. He is always with you, and whatever he allows you to go through is for your success and upliftment. After you have gone through the fire of the wilderness, He will promote and enthrone you. (1 Peter 5:10).

Every believer's faith cannot be strong until it is tested and approved by the fire of the wilderness. Paul, the apostle speaking to the Corinthians, said,' **"Every man's work shall be tested by fire, and every man's work that shall not be consumed by fire shall be rewarded".** No wonder Shedrack, Meshach and Abednego were immediately promoted after the fire in Babylon. If God is pleased to allow you to go through the fire in life, don't curse him, for there will always be a reason for it.

For He said to Jeremiah concerning the children of Israel

"I know the thoughts I think towards you; they are thoughts of good and not of evil to bring you to an expected end."

Jeremiah 29:II

We pray that whatever may be your wilderness, you shall never be discouraged until you inherit the promise after it. Mostly in the wilderness, friends can only comfort you, but don't expect help from any if they promise it. And don't blame them if they promise and fail because man cannot deliver you from God's wilderness of training unless your days of trial are over. Someone who knows where he/she is going will count it an opportunity that God almighty is training them up, though it is not always easy.

"My brethren, count it all joy when ye fall into divers temptations. Knowing this, that the trying of your faith worketh patience. But let patience have her perfect work that ye may be perfect and entire, wanting nothing."

James 1:2-4

"Cast not away therefore your confidence which hath great recompense of reward. For ye have need of patience that after ye have done the will of God, ye might receive the promise."

Hebrew 10:35-36

You can only receive the promise after you have done the will of God. The will of God is that you should endure trials because they are for your good. So Christians, never give up until God is through with you.

Chapter| 4

Endued with Power to Reign

Hast thou not known? Hast thou not heard? That the everlasting God the Lord, the creator of the ends of the earth, fainteth not? Neither is weary. There is no searching for His understanding. He giveth POWER to the faint to them that have no might he increaseth strength. Even the youths shall faint and be weary, and the young men shall utterly fall:
But they that wait upon the LORD shall renew their strength. They shall mount up with wings as eagles; They shall run and not be weary, and they shall walk and not faint.

Isaiah 40:28-31

Power is a commodity in the market that is in very high demand because of its unique functions. When you ask any reasonable person on the surface of the earth what is the most treasurable thing they have ever loved to have, they will tell you it is to have power and not only to have power but to be in power or have control over others. This means power is a necessity to everyone, not only in Christendom but to every single being occupying the surface of the earth. All over the world, there is a quest for power. Many even go to the level of killing so that they can reign. Praise the Lord. We are different species of humans that Jesus Christ, by death and resurrection, has introduced to a special kind of power which is unique and authentic in nature. When He died and resurrected, before ascending to heaven, he gave a commandment to those who have been with Him to tarry in Jerusalem until they are endued with divine energy to carry out the heavenly assignment on earth.

And behold, I send the promise of my father upon you but tarry ye in the city of Jerusalem until ye endued with power from on high. Luke 24:49

The word of God in the book of Ephesians 3:20 lets us understand that God is able to do exceeding abundantly, above all that we ever ask or imagine according to the power that is at work in our lives, which means your dimension of power will determine your achievements. The word power, as mentioned in Ephesians 3:20 from the Greek translation, means ***"Dunamis"***, denoting divine ability or enabling from the inside of a Christian that gives birth to a daily miraculous living. This means if you want to live miraculously on a daily basis, acquire the power, and the only means to acquire the power is to tarry or wait on the Lord. Waiting on the Lord involves the transformation period in the wilderness where God may allow the devil to test your ability in knowledge, understanding and the interpretation of biblical principles based on God's will.

And Jesus being full of the Holy Ghost returned from Jordan and was led by the spirit into the wilderness.

Being forty days tempted by the devil, He ate nothing in those days, and when they ended, He afterwards hungered.

And the devil said unto him, if thou be the son of God, command this stone that it be made bread.

Jesus answered him, saying that it was written that man should not leave by bread alone but by every word of God.

Luke 4:I-4

After this wilderness experience, Luke reports in the same chapter, in verse 37,

"And the fame of Him went out into every place of the country round about, which means after the trying moment in the wilderness, He was enthroned by God so much so that he became very famous all around the country."

The meaning of tarrying or waiting should not be limited to what happened in the upper room on the day of Pentecost because these guys in the upper room had been waiting for the fulfilment of the words of the master patiently for the last three and half years and Jesus telling them to wait was to fast. This was a way of telling them that it was time to receive what they had been waiting for. So, in the midst of your wilderness, if you go and close up yourself, feeling that is the way to end it, that will never be the solution. You have to be full of discerning ability so that you may be able to know what God wants you to do at a particular time because, without it, you will always be frustrated in the midst of the journey. A portion of the opening scripture reads,

"He giveth power to those that faint and to them that have no might He increaseth strength."

This means the weaker the vessel, the stronger the manifestation of the presence of God upon it. When you still have power and might of your own, God's power will be resting outside, but when your own energy and might are totally diminished, the power of God in you will rise to its full capacity. So if you are functioning in half power, it is evidence that your wilderness days are not over because the wilderness is the place of brokenness, and when you permit or allow the work to be fully done, He will make sure that your personality, self ambition are thwarted so that His perfect will can govern your life.

Chapter| 5
Walls of Fire

Season to Breaking out

"For you shall go out with joy and be led forth with peace: the mountains and the hills shall break forth before God in singing, and all the trees of the field shall clap their hands.
Instead of the thorns shall come up the fir tree, and instead of the brier shall come up the myrtle tree; and it shall be to the LORD for name, for an everlasting sign that shall not be cut off."

Isaiah 55:12-13

Brethren, there is an announcement from the throne of grace for you. No matter what your wilderness has been all this while, I want to assure you that sorrow may last for the night, but your day of Joy is coming with the morning. No matter the number of years you have spent in the wilderness, there is a promised land for you. God did not just take you out of Egypt to end your life in the desert. You have greater things to achieve beyond or within the walls of Jericho.

This special chapter begins with an announcement to you. For you shall go out with joy and be led forth with peace; the mountains and the hills shall break forth before you. When your set time of celebration, upliftment, and gratification comes, even the mountains and the hills that have been acting as hindrances to your progress and upliftment will have no choice but to act like your tools for the divine announcement, for the word of God says.

"They will break forth into singing and clapping for you when your joy and peace come.

When the Lord turned again to the captivity of Zion, we were like them in that dream.

Then was our mouth filled with laughter, and our tongue with singing: then said they among the heathen, the Lord has done great things for them.

The Lord has done great things for us, and we were glad."

Psalms 126:1-3

You must have been mourning for so long that you have forgotten that you can ever laugh again. Here, the word of God is assuring you that your lifting will be so great that the heathen shall announce the evidence; in other words, the unbelievers that have been mocking you and your God shall be the ones to sound the glorious breaking news of your breaking out into your land and realm of success and prosperity. The psalmist said, when the Lord turned again the captivity of Zion, we were like them that dream. The breaking of a new day is about to bring good news into your destiny. The Bible, from our opening scripture, says, "Instead of the thorns shall come forth the myrtle". This means your life of dryness will soon turn into your abundant land, a place of refuge and fruitfulness.

"You shall arise and have Mercy upon Zion for the time to favour her; yea, the set time is come. For your servants take pleasure in her stones and favour the dust thereof. So the heathens shall fear the name of the Lord and all the kings of the earth your glory. When the Lord shall build up Zion, he shall appear in his glory. He will regard the prayers of the destitute and not despise their prayers."

Psalms 102:13-15

"Christians, we want to let you know that all these years in the wilderness have been the plan of God so that He can be able to totally prune you up in preparation for you to inherit His promise for you, but now is your set time for Him to manifest His glory in your life in a greater dimension. Therefore

"Arise, shine, for your light comes and the glory of the Lord rises upon you for behold the darkness shall cover the earth and gross darkness the people but the Lord shall arise upon you and his glory shall be seen upon you and the Gentiles shall come to your light and kings to the brightness of your rising."

Isaiah 60: 1-3

Beloved, since you got born again, you have been groaning in darkness, but we are here to announce to you that there is an awesome visitation of light in your darkness that will act as a platform for divine publicity in your life. You shall be called great, for great men shall be your servants, and kings shall request for your friendship. Praise the Lord! Lift up your voice now and say,

"This is my time of greatness; I am breaking out of difficulties; My life is taking another dimension this season. Amen."

Your time of incubation is over. A fowl cannot stay beyond twenty-one days in its shell, so this is your due season for breaking out. Your ninth month of being pregnant with greatness is over, and you are due for delivery. Babylon is not your final destination. The Lord must have allowed you in the hand of your enemy to torture you, but this is your season of breaking out of that bondage, for this Word is coming to you to prosper you in your land of adversity. Listen to what the Lord said through Jeremiah to those that He allowed to be carried to captivity in the land of Babylon.

Thus says the LORD of hosts, the God of Israel, to all that are carried away captives whom I have caused to be carried from Jerusalem to Babylon. Build your houses and dwell in them, plant gardens, and eat their fruits.

Take you wives and father sons and daughters and take wives for your sons and give your daughters to husbands, that they may bear sons and daughters that you may increase there and not diminish and seek the peace of the city where I have caused you to be carried away captives and pray to the LORD for it for in the peace thereof shall you have peace.

For thus says the LORD of hosts, the GOD of Israel, let not your prophets and your diviners that be in the midst of you deceive you neither hearken to your dreams which you cause to be dreamed.

For they prophesy falsely to you in my name: I have not sent them, says the Lord. For thus says the LORD that after seventy years be accomplished at Babylon, I will visit you and perform my good word towards you in causing you to return to this place.

For I know the thoughts I think towards you says the LORD thoughts of peace and not of evil to give you an expected end.

Then shall you call upon me, and you shall go and pray to me, and I will hearken to you. And you shall seek me and find me when you shall search for me with all your heart, and I will be found of you says the LORD, and I will them away your captivity and I will gather you from all the nations and from all places where I have driven you says the LORD and I will bring you again into this place where I caused you to be carried away captive.

Jeremiah 29:4-14

There was a reason He allowed you in that wilderness, and there was also a set time in His book of record to allow you to break forth. He is telling you that all that He is doing to you, whether you consider it evil or good, all such as many of them as have been your encounter, have been working for your good, and this is your set time of breaking out. Babylon is not your eternal home but Jerusalem. We announce to you that you are breaking out of Babylon into your promised home in Jerusalem.

Chapter| 6
Fire and Sacrifice

Now Moses kept the Flock of Jethro, his father-in-law, the priest of Median, and he came to the mountain of God, even Horeb.

And the angel of the Lord appeared unto him in a flame of fire out of the midst of the bush, and he looked and behold the bush burned with fire, but the bush was not consumed.

And Moses said I would now turn aside and see this great sight of why the bush is not burnt.

And when the Lord saw that he turned aside to see, God called unto him out of the midst of the bush and said, Moses, Moses, and he said, here am I.

And He said draw not nigh hither, put off thy shoes from off thy feet for the place whereon thou standest is holy ground.

Exodus 3:1-5

Fire produces light. Moses has been working in Jethro's house for over forty years now as a shepherd, and God, this time around, had to redirect his purpose and destiny. When the Lord appeared to Moses in the midst of the burning bush, He told Moses to take off his shoes, giving him reasons that he was standing on holy ground. Normally, the pair of shoes Moses was wearing was made of leather. The reason for the removal of these leather shoes was that they acted as insulators between Moses and the presence of God on this mountain. So God wanted Moses to take off the shoes so that he could have a direct encounter with his divine presence. It was only after Moses put off the shoes that God started speaking to him and explained to him the purpose for his sudden visitation, after which we are told from the bible God wrought a great deal of miracles through Moses. The primary purpose of fire was to burn out every form of filthiness in the life of Moses. All that would have disqualified him from receiving this noble assignment from the Lord.

Moses was to be a light to radiate from Egypt to the Land of Promise, so every filthiness was supposed to be burnt out of his life so that God could use him as a source of light to them. Just as Moses removed the sandals from his feet before God could start speaking to him and revealing the purpose of his sudden visitation, there are some issues in your life that when God wants to send you on assignment, He must make sure that they are totally burnt out.

This is why on the Pentecost day, the bible truly reveals to us that certain flames like cloven tongues of fire appeared upon the disciples in the upper room. And when the day of Pentecost was fully come they were all with one accord in one place and suddenly there came a sound from heaven as of a rushing mighty wind and it filled all the house where they were sitting.

And there appeared unto them coven tongues like as of fire, and it sat upon each of them.

And they were all filled with the Holy Ghost and began to speak with other tongues as the Spirit gave them utterance.

On the day of Pentecost, after cloven tongues like those of fire sat upon the followers of Jesus Christ the bibletells us that they were filled with the spirit whom the father gave them, enabling to speak in different tongues.

The cloven tongues were a symbol of fire of purification. God used His fire to purify them so that their bodies could be habitable to Him. Furthermore, when their bodies were cleansed and habitable, the

Lord came into their lives through the presence of the Holy Spirit and filled them so that their tongues could worship the Lord in sincerity.

For then, I will turn to the people a pure language that they may call upon the name of the Lord to serve him in one consent.

Zephaniah 3:9

Every sacrifice that must be accepted must pass through fire. Fire discipline brings self-denial, self-control, and life that is not controlled by the flesh because the fire burns out every flesh and self-ego. When you go through the fire experience, you become a lighthouse to the world. The Bible says,

"For so hath the Lord commanded us saying I have set thee to be light of the Gentiles, that thou shouldest be for salvation unto the ends of the earth."

Act. 13:47

The Lord uses the fire experience to make you a useful, usable, pliable and qualified sacrifice on His altar so that you can be a lighthouse aglow with the gospel of Jesus Christ. Little wonder Jesus Christ said**, "Ye are the Light of the world. A city that is set on a hill cannot be hidden" (Matthew 5:14).** God wants you to go through the fire on the altar of His sacrifice so that you can be a lighthouse to the Gentiles and the kings.

He also intends that after you have been offered as a sacrifice on His altar, your light beam will radiate at a higher frequency and cause those in darkness to become light to others. The Holy Ghost fashions you to be a light Channel to your World.

"Arise, (therefore and) shine for thy light is come and the glory of the Lord is risen upon thee.

For, behold the darkness shall cover the earth, and gross darkness the people, but the LORD shall arise upon you, and His glory shall be seen upon you.
And the gentiles shall come to thy light, and kings to the brightness of your rising."

Isaiah 60: I-3

No matter what you are going through, I want to use this medium to announce to you that you are a channel of light waiting to be switched on in its season. Do not ever allow darkness to over shadow your knowledge of who you are to the world. You are a light to it and it is now totally your responsibility to get your light shine or to allow yourself in darkness. But I will rather advise you to get a revelation that will illuminate your life forever.

Let your light shine before men so that they may see your good works and glorify your father, who is in heaven.

Matthew 5:16

The Bible says; let one's light shine. It was a command and not a proposal, or neither was it a request, which means the level at which your light is going to shine is totally determined by how much you are going to let it shine and how much you are going to let it shine is totally determined on how much energy you are going to acquire for it, and how much energy you are going to acquire for it is based in your spirit man.

And to know the Love of Christ that passes knowledge that ye might be filled with all the fullness of God. Now unto him that is able to do exceeding, abundantly, above all that, we ask or think according to the power that works in us.

Ephesians 3:19-20

And such as have done wickedly against the Lord shall he corrupt by flatteries, but the people that do know their God shall be strong and do exploit.

Daniel 11:32

We first read two powerful scriptures talking about knowledge and power. Exploit doing is based on the quality and quantity of knowledge you have in your spirit. God is willing to make known to you the riches of the word and glory, but you have a personal choice to make, and this choice is to live a consistent and persistent Christian life by presenting. You are on the altar to be slammed by his fire so that you can have a deeper knowledge of His will for you.

I beseech you, therefore brethren, by the mercies of God that ye present your bodies a living sacrifice, holy and acceptable unto God, which is your reasonable service.

And be not conformed to this world but be transformed by the renewing of your mind, that ye may prove, what is that good, and acceptable and perfect will of God.

Romans 12:1-2

We are made to understand that when we present our bodies as a living sacrifice, we will be acceptable to God when our sacrifice is holy. Interestingly the Father tells us that after presenting our bodies as an acceptable holy sacrifice to God, we should be transformed rather than conforming to this world. This is to grant us the divine ability to prove that; which is the good, acceptable and God's perfect will for us.

This is to say, by knowledge and understanding, we can totally prove and establish His perfect will for you before the world begins. Knowledge is paramount for our success and the manifestation of God's presence in our lives. It is impossible to manifest the glory of God in our lives, careers, and ministries beyond the revelation and information in our knowledge box. Therefore, to aspire to greater heights and notable achievements in our lives, careers and destinies, we are required to be constant researchers and Bible students. The mysteries that have been hidden for ages and from generations are made manifest to His saints through deep knowledge and understanding.

"To whom God would make known what the riches of the glory of this mystery among the Gentiles are, Christ in you, the hope of glory.

Whom we preach, warning every man, and teaching every man in all wisdom, that we may present every man perfect in Christ Jesus."

Colossians I:26-28

Brethren, there is a mystery about the sacrifice that was offered at Calvary. Understanding it will expose us to the glory of God. One significant thing that we will also want to emphasize is that the greater, higher, and deeper we gain an understanding of this mystery, the greater our glory radiates at a much higher frequency. The deeper we go in this mystery, the higher our operation in God's glory. Praise the Lord. We counsel you to keep thirsting and going after the higher revelation in God through Christ Jesus.

Chapter| 7
Prophetic Declarations

- This is my season of divine explosion.
- In this season, I declare that my family and I will overcome challenges and poverty in the name of Jesus Christ.
- My set time of favour has come, and no one is permitted to deprive me of my Godly heritage and blessings.
- I am a miracle waiting to happen in Jesus' name.
- I declare that I can never stop halfway in my destiny journey in Jesus' Name.
- I decree and declare that the walls of fire are consuming every evil gate in my life and family.
- I am too anointed to be a disappointment in my generation.
- I declare failure is a stranger in my affairs of life
- No weapon, formed and fashioned against me, shall ever prosper, for that is my heritage as a child of God.
- I decree that I am living an ever-increasing life- forward ever and backwards never.
- I declare that I can never be confused, frustrated and downcast anywhere I go, for the spirit of the Lord is upon me.
- I decree super intelligence and divine wisdom in everything I do to the glory of God in Jesus' name.

- This is my season of proof and testimonies in whatsoever I lay my hands to do in Jesus' name.
- I decree supper abundance is my portion in any domain of my life in Jesus' name.
- I decree that my destiny is surrounded by walls of fire against every wind of evil in Jesus' name.
- I declare that everything about my life shall be extraordinary this season in Jesus' name.
- I am increasing in knowledge and revelation of Jesus Christ's name
- I am light to the world, for my father is the giver of light
- I can never die in my wilderness, for there is a throne waiting for me in Jesus' name.
- I declare that l am increasing in the supernatural and reducing in the natural in Jesus' name.
- I declare that I live beyond every human suggestion and opinion, for l am a product of the supernatural.
- I decree and declare I can never be a liability forever.
- This season, I will lend to many nations, but I shall not borrow.
- I declare, by knowledge, I am increasing in the anointing power of God
- I decree and declare that my financial resources are from above; therefore, no weapon fashioned against my success shall prosper in Jesus' name.
- I shall not continue to have a life of wants, for the Lord is the shepherd over my entire life.
- I am making spiritual advancement, and I declare that I am unstoppable in all my spiritual adventures.
- I am mounting up with the wings of the eagle to be repositories above and never beneath again in my life.
- I declare that in this season, I am prospering in all my heart desires in Jesus' name.

- I declare that this season is my season of change and upliftment. The Iron Maker is removing any iron gate that has been obstructing my life, in Jesus' name.

Chapter| 8
Formatting

Formatting in a computer or any electronic system is the process whereby irrelevant information is deleted from the system to allow it to be empty so that it can be able to carry new updates or data. In like manner, this unique chapter will explain to us how our lives can go through the process of formatting so that we can become brand-new Christians. We will also explain to you the various sources of formatting and our individual responsibilities in this project.

For of the blood of bulls and of goats and ashes of a higher sprinkling the unclean, santifieth to the purifying of the flesh.

How much more shall the blood of Christ who through the Eternal Spirit offers Himself without spot to God, purge your conscience from death works to serve the living God.

Hebrews 9:13-14

The Bible says Jesus Christ, through the eternal spirit, offered himself to God without spot to purge or cleanse our conscience from dead works so that we can be able to serve the living God, which means without Christ offering himself to God and cleansing our conscience from dead works, we wouldn't have been able to serve God in sincerity. That explains to us that there were a lot of issues in our conscience that Jesus Christ needed to, **by the spirit format**, delete, purge, or cleanse before we could fully derive freedom in our spirit to serve the living God.

The generation of Moses could not enter the Promised Land while in the wilderness because they kept reminding themselves of the evil pleasures of Egypt. While they were walking towards the Promised Land, their minds were still full of Egypt. They had the mentality of the Egyptians, and God couldn't take Israelites with Egyptian mentalities to inherit the promise because the promise was supposed to be inherited by the Israelites. Joshua and Caleb, from whom the spirit had deleted (formatted) every Egyptian mentality, were given a new vision for the Promised Land.

Surely they shall not see the land which I sware unto their fathers, neither shall any of them that provoke me to see it. But my servant Caleb, because he had ANOTHER spirit with him, will I bring into the land whereinto he went, and his seed shall possess it.

Numbers 14:23-24

The Bible also spoke of Joshua, saying
"And Joshua the son of Nun was full of the spirit of wisdom; for Moses has laid his hands upon him and the children of Israel hearkened unto him and did as the LORD commanded Moses"

Deuteronomy 34:9

Six hundred thousand humans embarked on a journey to the promised land, and only two people, Joshua and Caleb, amongst those who set out for this journey, arrived at the prophesied destination. The word of God explains to us that it was because these two guys were filled with the spirit of God. Come to think of this. Was it that all of these Six hundred thousand people were not morally upgraded? No, we do not share such views because the bible informed us that those who entered this land were filled with the spirit of God. This means we can only access God's promise for us when the Holy Spirit must have completed some formatting work in our lives. This is so because **new wine cannot be preserved in old wineskins.** Any such attempt will burst the old wineskins and waste the content. Therefore, **through the formatting process, God will fully prepare new wineskins for the preservation of His new wine (new potentials, new life, new talents, etc.)**

Now the works of the flesh are manifest, which are these: adultery, fornication, uncleanliness, lasciviousness, idolatry, witchcraft, hatred variance, emulation, wrath, strife, seductive heresies, envying, murders, drunkenness, revelling and such like: of the which I tell you before, as I have also told you in time past, that they which do such things shall not inherit the kingdom of God.

But the fruit of the spirit is love, joy, peace, longsuffering, gentleness, goodness, faith, meekness, temperance against such there is no law. And they that are Christ's have crucified the flesh with the affections and lust.

Galatians 5:19-24

From verses 19-21 of this scripture, we are informed of what the natural man or men in the flesh will do. Normally, when one is living a life in the flesh, it will be impossible for such a person to escape all of such works of the flesh and those works that are against the presence of God in every life.

"For the flesh lusteth against the spirit, and the spirit lusteth against the flesh, these are contrary to one another, so that ye cannot do the things that ye would.

But if ye be led of the Spirit, ye are not under the law."

Galatians 5:17-18

This scripture tells us that we are no longer under the law when the spirit leads us. This means that a spirit-filled

Christian will naturally exercise the fruit of the spirit as outlined in Galatians 5:22-24 without being obliged by the law of Moses. Formatting takes a process. It is not a day's job. Where God is taking us will determine the formatting process. There are things that God can use to format our fathers' houses. There are others whom He will use the prison so that at the end you can speak like Joseph to the brothers from the prime minister's throne in Egypt. **"And he wept aloud, and the Egyptians and the house of Pharaoh heard."**

And Joseph said to his brethren, "I am Joseph: doth my father yet live? And his brethren could not answer him, for they were troubled in his presence."

And Joseph said to his brethren, "Come near I pray you, and they came near, and he said, I am Joseph, your brother whom ye sold into Egypt.

Now, therefore, be not grieved nor angry with yourselves that ye sold me hither, for God did send me before you to preserve life."

Genesis 45:2-5

In other words, Joseph appreciates his brethren for allowing God to use them as formatting agencies to prepare him for the throne in Egypt. It did not end there. He invited them to come to Egypt and enjoy the fruit of their labour. So, brothers, do not be angry when you are overtaken by an ugly event in your journey in life. It may be your brothers or even associates who knock at you in the process; do not be dismayed because God is preparing you to bless them!

We sincerely hope that you are blessed by reading this exposition. May the Lord continue to protect you, your family and associates with His Wall of Fire in Jesus' Name. Amen!

www.ingramcontent.com/pod-product-compliance
Lightning Source LLC
Chambersburg PA
CBHW050026170726
48282CB00025B/561